The Lincoln Memorial

by Kristin L. Nelson

PULL AHEAD BOOKS
American Symbols

Lerner Publications Company • Minneapolis

To anyone who has fought for something he or she deeply believed in

This book is available in two editions:
Library binding by Lerner Publications Company, a division of Lerner Publishing Group, Inc.
Soft cover by First Avenue Editions, an imprint of Lerner Publishing Group, Inc.
241 First Avenue North
Minneapolis, MN 55401 U.S.A.

Website address: www.lernerbooks.com

Words in **bold type** are explained in a glossary on page 31.

Library of Congress Cataloging-in-Publication Data

Nelson, Kristin L.
    The Lincoln Memorial / by Kristin L. Nelson.
       p.   cm. — (Pull ahead books)
    Summary: Describes the significance, history, and
construction of the Lincoln Memorial.
    Includes index.
    ISBN-13: 978–0–8225–3690–1 (lib. bdg. : alk. paper)
    ISBN-10: 0–8225–3690–0 (lib. bdg. : alk. paper)
    ISBN-13: 978–0–8225–3761–8 (pbk. : alk. paper)
    ISBN-10: 0–8225–3761–3 (pbk. : alk. paper)
    1. Lincoln Memorial (Washington, D.C.)—Juvenile
literature. 2. Lincoln, Abraham, 1809–1865—Monuments—
Juvenile literature. 3. Washington (D.C.)—Buildings,
structures, etc.—Juvenile literature. [1. Lincoln Memorial
(Washington, D.C.) 2. National monuments.] I. Title.
II. Series.
F203.4.L73N45 2004
973.7'092—dc21   2003000385

Manufactured in the United States of America
7 – CG – 3/1/10

What building in Washington, D.C.,
has **marble** steps leading up to it?

It is the Lincoln Memorial. A **memorial** is something that helps us remember a person who died.

The Lincoln Memorial was built to help people remember **President** Abraham Lincoln.

Abraham Lincoln became a hero to many people. He led the United States through a very hard time.

In the 1800s, most African Americans were **slaves.** Lincoln thought slavery was wrong. He believed that every American should be free.

Some people agreed with Lincoln. Others did not. In 1861, the **Civil War** started between these two groups.

After four years, the war ended.
Lincoln had kept the country together.
He made slavery against the law.

Some people did not like the president's ideas. On April 14, 1865, a man shot Lincoln. The president died the next day.

People were sad about their leader's death. Many wanted to build a memorial.

The memorial would be a **symbol** of Lincoln's fight to keep his nation together. It would stand for his work to free the slaves.

In 1914, workers started building the memorial. They used a hard stone called marble.

The workers put 36 **columns** around the building. Columns are shaped like thick poles. Together they hold up the building.

The columns in the Lincoln Memorial stand for the states. There were 36 states when Lincoln died.

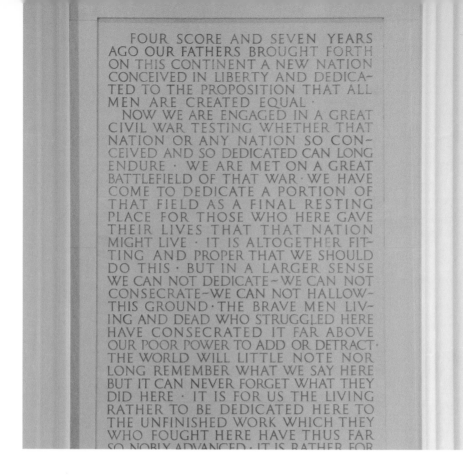

FOUR SCORE AND SEVEN YEARS
AGO OUR FATHERS BROUGHT FORTH
ON THIS CONTINENT A NEW NATION
CONCEIVED IN LIBERTY AND DEDICA-
TED TO THE PROPOSITION THAT ALL
MEN ARE CREATED EQUAL ·
NOW WE ARE ENGAGED IN A GREAT
CIVIL WAR TESTING WHETHER THAT
NATION OR ANY NATION SO CON-
CEIVED AND SO DEDICATED CAN LONG
ENDURE · WE ARE MET ON A GREAT
BATTLEFIELD OF THAT WAR · WE HAVE
COME TO DEDICATE A PORTION OF
THAT FIELD AS A FINAL RESTING
PLACE FOR THOSE WHO HERE GAVE
THEIR LIVES THAT THAT NATION
MIGHT LIVE · IT IS ALTOGETHER FIT-
TING AND PROPER THAT WE SHOULD
DO THIS · BUT IN A LARGER SENSE
WE CAN NOT DEDICATE ~ WE CAN NOT
CONSECRATE ~ WE CAN NOT HALLOW ~
THIS GROUND · THE BRAVE MEN LIV-
ING AND DEAD WHO STRUGGLED HERE
HAVE CONSECRATED IT FAR ABOVE
OUR POOR POWER TO ADD OR DETRACT ·
THE WORLD WILL LITTLE NOTE NOR
LONG REMEMBER WHAT WE SAY HERE
BUT IT CAN NEVER FORGET WHAT THEY
DID HERE · IT IS FOR US THE LIVING
RATHER TO BE DEDICATED HERE TO
THE UNFINISHED WORK WHICH THEY
WHO FOUGHT HERE HAVE THUS FAR
SO NOBLY ADVANCED · IT IS RATHER FOR

Parts of President Lincoln's famous speeches appear on the walls inside the memorial.

There are murals above the speeches. A mural is a large picture painted on a wall.

A **statue** of President Lincoln sits in the center of the memorial.

A sculptor named Daniel Chester French made the statue. A sculptor carves objects out of wood or stone.

French carved the statue from 28 pieces of marble. He put these pieces together like parts of a puzzle.

The statue was 19 feet tall when it was finished. That is as tall as three men standing on each other's shoulders!

In 1922, the Lincoln Memorial was complete.

The memorial became a place for people to come together. Some people gave speeches there.

In 1963, Martin Luther King Jr. gave a speech on the steps of the memorial.

He told Americans about his dream
that all people would one day have
freedom and equal rights.

The Lincoln Memorial is still a place for people to gather and talk about their hopes and ideas.

It reminds us of President Lincoln's work
to keep the United States together.
And it stands for his hope that its
people will always be free.

Facts about the Lincoln Memorial

■ Workers started building the memorial on February 12, 1914. That day would have been Abraham Lincoln's 105th birthday!

■ The pool in front of the memorial is almost one-third of a mile long!

■ To make the statue of Lincoln, Daniel Chester French used molds of Lincoln's hands and face. A mold is a copy of the shape of something. The molds were made when Lincoln was alive.

■ The statue shows Lincoln's right hand open. This stands for his care for others. Lincoln's closed left hand is a symbol of his power as the president.

■ The murals in the Lincoln Memorial are each 60 feet long and 12 feet tall.

■ Lincoln's son Robert Todd was the guest of honor at the memorial's opening in 1922.

Marian Anderson

In 1939, a famous African American singer named Marian Anderson wanted to sing at Constitution Hall in Washington, D.C. But, at this time, African Americans were often not allowed to go to places kept for white people. The owners of Constitution Hall would not let Marian sing in their hall.

Many people heard this news and were angry. Some of these people set up a concert for Marian at the Lincoln Memorial. About 75,000 people came to hear her sing on the steps of the memorial. This concert became a symbol of the fight for equality. Four years later, Marian was invited to sing at Constitution Hall.

More about the Lincoln Memorial

D'Aulaire, Ingri and Edgar D'Aulaire. *Abraham Lincoln.* New York: Doubleday, 1939.

Mattern, Joanne. *Young Martin Luther King Jr.: "I Have a Dream."* Mahwah, N.J.: Troll Publishing, 1992.

Ryan, Pam Muñoz. *When Marian Sang.* New York: Scholastic, Inc., 2002.

Schott, Jane A. *Abraham Lincoln.* Minneapolis, MN: Lerner Publishing Group, 2002.

Websites

Ben's Guide to U.S. Government for Kids–Symbols of U.S. Government
http://bensguide.gpo.gov/3-5/symbols/

National Park Service: Lincoln Memorial
http://www.nps.gov/linc/index.htm

Visiting the Lincoln Memorial
The Lincoln Memorial is located on the west end of the National Mall in Washington, D.C. It is open to visitors every day except Christmas.

Glossary

Civil War: A war between two groups of people in one country. In the 1860s, the people living in the North of the United States fought those living in the South.

columns: tall supports for a building

marble: a hard stone with colored patterns used for buildings and sculptures

memorial: a place, event, or thing that helps remind us of a person who died

president: the leader of a country, such as the United States

slaves: people forced to work without pay

statue: a copy carved in stone or wood of a person or thing

symbol: an object that stands for an idea, a country, or a person

Index

Photo Acknowledgments

The pictures in this book have been reproduced with the permission of: Library of Congress, pp. 3, 5, 6, 7, 9, 10, 13, 21, 22, 24; © A. A. M. Van der Heyden/Independent Picture Service, p. 4; © Leib Image Archives, p. 8; Argosy Bookstore, New York, p. 11; © North Wind Picture Archives, p. 12; © Margo Taussig Pinkerton/Photo Network, pp. 14, 15; © Jay Mallin, pp. 16, 17, 26; © Henryk T. Kaiser/Photo Network, p.18; *Dictionary of American Portraits,* p. 19; National Archives, pp. 20, 23; © Hulton-Deutsch Collection/CORBIS, p. 25; © Lonnie Duka/Photo Network, p. 27; © Bettmann/CORBIS, p. 29.

Cover photo used with the permission of: © Henryk T. Kaiser/Photo Network.